LINCOLN CHRISTIA P9-CDF-117

What Is Worship Music?

Basics of the Faith

How Do We Glorify God?
How Our Children Come to Faith
What Are Election and Predestination?
What Is a Reformed Church?
What Is a True Calvinist?
What Is Biblical Preaching?
What Is Church Government?
What Is Hell?
What Is Justification by Faith Alone?
What Is Perseverance of the Saints?
What Is Providence?
What Is Spiritual Warfare?
What Is the Christian Worldview?
What Is the Lord's Supper?
What Is True Conversion?
What Is Vocation?
What Is Worship Music?
Why Do We Baptize Infants?

What Is Worship Music?

Paul S. Jones

P&R
PUBLISHING
P.O. BOX 817 • PHILLIPSBURG • NEW JERSEY 08865-0817

© 2010 by Paul Steven Jones

All rights reserved. No part of this book may be reproduced, stored in a retrieval system, or transmitted in any form or by any means—electronic, mechanical, photocopy, recording, or otherwise—except for brief quotations for the purpose of review or comment, without the prior permission of the publisher, P&R Publishing Company, P.O. Box 817, Phillipsburg, New Jersey 08865-0817.

Unless otherwise indicated, Scripture quotations are from *ESV Bible* ® (*The Holy Bible, English Standard Version* ®). Copyright © 2001 by Crossway Bibles, a publishing ministry of Good News Publishers. Used by permission. All rights reserved.

Italics within Scripture quotations indicate emphasis added.

Page design by Tobias Design

Printed in the United States of America

Library of Congress Cataloging-in-Publication Data

Jones, Paul S., 1969-
  What is worship music? / Paul S. Jones.
      p. cm. -- (Basics of the faith)
  Includes bibliographical references.
  ISBN 978-1-59638-198-8 (pbk.)
  1. Music--Religious aspects--Christianity. 2. Church music. 3. Music in churches. I. Title.
  ML3001.J664 2010
  264'.2--dc22
                              2010010200

■What is worship music? Can it be defined? Does the Bible tell us? Does it exist in one acceptable style, or two, or three? Is any music with Christian words acceptable?

One would be hard-pressed to find definitive answers to these questions by observing practices in the church today. Currently, it seems, each assembly does what is right in its own eyes. Our relativistic, pluralistic society embraces everything, and the church follows closely on its heels. Often we are too inclusive, sometimes too exclusive. Many churches today prefer spontaneity to providing order for the reverent and thoughtful worship of God. One would expect churches that claim to value the authority of Scripture to follow biblical principles for worship—but do they? And is there anything that we can learn about biblical worship from church history? The Reformers gave great attention to liturgy, carefully considering worship elements and their order; so yes, we can.

Worship music is at the center of controversy, being one of the most divisive issues in the church, as it has been for decades. Somehow we have come to define worship services almost exclusively on the basis of musical style. "Contemporary," "traditional," "blended," or "classical" worship services receive their labels from the type of music included and that music's accoutrements, which can run the gamut from

122493

liturgical robes and pipe organs to flip-flops and digital drum sets. While legitimate differences exist in the music of various people groups, the postmodern church has tended toward "pop" culture as its pragmatic answer for music, and toward youth pop culture in particular. I fear that this is an enormous mistake. We need to be following biblical principles for worship music, not the world, youth culture, or ideas based on mistaken notions of success.

In some places, biblical worship principles are entirely ignored; in many others, they have not been thoroughly explored. And there is little wonder how this came to be. Protestant seminaries exclude virtually any musical training for pastors, even though churches depend on ministers to set good practices for them. Christian colleges and universities have watered down their music programs to meet the felt needs of their constituents (to stay fiscally viable) rather than training the next generation to lead the church in better directions. The church itself has become increasingly worldly, and we have forgotten the legacy the Reformers left to us.

Consumerism tells us that if we are "paying," we should get what we want. So congregational factions and individuals wrestle for equal representation or dominance, to ensure that their musical desires are satisfied in the church where they are "customers," whether or not they are members. Trained church musicians are frequently forced to take liberal church posts to survive because conservative churches, by and large, do not value, hire, or support them. Amateurs end up leading worship music when and where they should not, sometimes by default, sometimes by design.

The result: church music is adrift in a sea of trends, being blown about by the wind of every opinion, regardless of how modestly informed these may be. Many well-meaning people, including musicians and pastors, misuse music in worship unknowingly. Some individuals and organizations profit through its increasing commercialization, while many churches are shortchanged by the shallowness and man-centeredness that characterize much so-called worship today. Yes, the worship-music seascape is rather bleak. We can navigate through this muddle back to solid ground, however, if we are searching for truth. God's Word provides answers.

Based on biblical evidence, music properly fulfills three roles in the context of worship: *praise*, *prayer*, and *proclamation*. *Praise* is the lauding of God for his acts and attributes, acknowledging his supremacy in all things. *Prayer* is communication addressed to God. *Proclamation* encompasses any activity that proclaims the Word of God—quotation, explanation, teaching, and preaching. Praise, prayer, and proclamation are the roles of psalmody and hymnody, of vocal music and instrumental music. They extend to congregation and choir, to layperson and minister, to organist and guitarist. And *when worship music is properly fulfilling these roles according to biblical principles*, discord dissipates, unity increases, and the Spirit utilizes music for its highest purpose, for man's chief purpose—to glorify the triune God.

For our worship music to be biblical, it must find its themes, principles, and qualities in Scripture. Careful consideration and implementation of what God has revealed will correct aberrations in practice. This short volume seeks to interact with biblical evidence concerning music in order to arrive at biblical principles for the local church.[1] We briefly revisit the thinking of leading Protestant Reformers on the topic of music as well. Our goals are the glory of God and the edification of the church as we reconsider one of the greatest gifts bestowed on us by our beneficent God, and its application to our present and future chief occupation—worshiping him.

WORSHIP MUSIC IS PRAISE

It Is a Biblical Response to God's Person, Works, and Word

My lips will pour forth praise, for you teach me your statutes. (Psalm 119:171)

No one questions the idea that worship music is used to praise God. In fact, some people I know refer to all the musical elements of worship as "the praise" even when music may be serving multiple roles. Others mistakenly call it "praise and worship," as if those terms somehow designated distinct categories of music, different types of activity, or a genre. We hear phrases such as *praise songs*, *praise teams*, and *praise bands* applied to musical forms and ensembles, with the connotation that praise is the sole function of such entities. Certainly the praise of God is a leading role of music in worship, and the majority of biblical songs contain elements of praise even if praise is not their primary theme. But this is not music's only function.

Praise-infused biblical songs include several genres. In addition to the canonical psalms (which range from praise to lament to the recounting of history), there are major and minor canticles, hymns of Christ, and doxologies. A brief look at these biblical songs grants insight into concepts and content that should characterize the songs we sing in worship. We should also note that because these biblical songs are the very Word of God, they are part of our spiritual birthright. They should have a significant place in our collective repertoire, starting with the psalms.

Psalms

The canonical Psalter has been the principal source of worship music for God's people for millennia. The function of psalms in worship changed throughout Israel's temple history, and their employment in the synagogue and the New Testament church was transformed as well. Psalms were understood as praise when first used in Israel's worship. Later, the two chief occasions on which psalms were sung in Solomon's temple were upon entering and at the immolation of the sacrifice. In the synagogue, the psalms became spiritual sacrifices (1 Peter 2:5), since the system of animal sacrifices was no longer in place.[2]

The early church kept many synagogue traditions; one of these was the singing of psalms in the context of prayer. According to Hughes Oliphant Old, Psalm 118:27 provides a good example of the changing use of psalms: "Bind the festal sacrifice with cords, up to the horns of the altar!" In temple worship, this action was literal; the animal would have been bound. In synagogue worship, this was symbolic. In the early church, this verse would have been understood as a celebration of Christ's death and resurrection.[3] Christ had fulfilled God's demand for blood sacrifice, thereby abolishing the need for this practice in worship.

Psalm-singing is commanded as part of New Testament worship in Ephesians 5:19 and Colossians 3:16.[4] These passages direct us to sing psalms, hymns, and spiritual songs (or odes). Some have argued that the three designations are simply interchangeable words for canonical psalms, pointing out that the Septuagint uses all three words in psalm subtitles. Thus, these were terms with which Paul and believers of his day would have been familiar.[5] Wesley Isenberg writes that

> the very use of diverse terminology such as this suggests that the early Church encouraged a creative variety of musical and poetic expression in its corporate

worship. Had the Church sought to discourage such expression, the variety of terms would eventually have given way to a single term, by which we would now be able to define and delimit the "hymn form."[6]

Irrespective of one's conclusion about these verses, singing psalms is not optional; yet the practice is missing from many worship services. It is insufficient to sing a chorus based on a psalm verse and ignore the reasons the psalm gives for worshiping God. Such reasons should be recalled if our thanks, praise, and prayers to God are to be properly contextualized and purposeful. Aim to include at least one psalm in every worship service.

John Calvin and Psalm Singing

Upon his June 1536 arrival in Geneva, John Calvin established daily gatherings for psalm singing and expository preaching.[7] He and fellow Reformer Guillaume Farel agreed that the congregation should be singing psalms, so they requested this of the City Council. The Council concurred but was slow to act. When the Reformers were expelled from Geneva in 1538 on another matter, congregational singing was still not common practice. At this point Calvin went to Strasbourg, where he encountered Martin Bucer (1491–1551), who invited Calvin to pastor the French refugee church there.

Bucer's German church included congregational singing on a grand scale, with two thousand persons of all ages singing psalms and hymns under the direction of a precentor (lead singer/choir director/teacher), who led his choir of schoolchildren to aid the congregation. This must have been a moving experience for Calvin. In Roman churches of the time, priests chanted in Latin, and choirs of professional singers sang Latin polyphonic music. Worship services did not include congregational song or any other music in the common tongue. Martin Luther had given German Protestant churches chorales (hymns) to sing. The *Strasbourg German Service Book* of 1537 integrated all 150 psalms with festal hymns, morning and evening hymns, and catechetical hymns, including some of Luther's.[8]

Calvin decided that something similar needed to happen in French churches. And so, through the *Strasbourg Psalter* and the various iterations of the *Genevan* (or *Huguenot*) *Psalter*, he delivered (with the aid of skilled poets and musicians) the complete canonical psalms, as well as a few hymns, to the francophone church. He prescribed that these worship songs should be sung in unison, without instrumental accompaniment, led by a children's choir under the direction of a precentor. The psalms were sung in the early-church modes (types of musical scales) on a rotating schedule in all Sunday morning/evening and Wednesday evening services of the Genevan churches. They were included as a worship element in their own right, not specifically linked to the sermon of the day, as a form of prayer.

Psalms Only?

The canonical psalms are not the only appropriate worship songs of the people of God; the Bible provides other songs as well. New Testament examples show that worship should also include our Christian response to the finished work of Calvary. This could be called a "Christian interpretation of the psalms" through hymns, canticles, and other biblical songs. The Word of God also commands us to sing "new" songs (e.g., Ps. 149:1). According to Old, "the doxology of the earliest Christians kept psalmody and hymnody in a dynamic balance."[9] Without Christian hymns, our praise of God through the psalms would be rich, but it would be missing our acknowledgment of and gratitude for Christ's redemption and his fulfillment of Old Testament promises. In fact, since the second century in many traditions, the *Gloria Patri*, a Christian doxology, has been added to the end of psalms sung in worship to underscore the revealed Trinitarian nature of God.

Calvin wrote hymns and included them in his psalters (e.g., Ten Commandments, Apostles' Creed, Song of Simeon), so he cannot be called an "exclusive psalmodist," though many choose to describe him as such. The Westminster Confession (1646) does not mention hymns and spiritual songs when it refers to "singing of psalms with grace in the heart" (chapter 21:5). But Robert Rayburn rightly notes, "This omission does not mean that we should sing the Old Testament psalms only. The Confession uses the word in a wider sense to refer to hymns sung to God."[10] Old clearly states, "The continental Reformers did not argue for exclusive psalmody. Several of the early Reformed churches published worship books that offered not only psalms, but hymns and spiritual songs as well."[11] In fact, the *Constance Hymn Book* of 1540 was almost equally made up of psalms and hymns.[12]

For a discussion of exclusive psalmody, I refer the reader to Vern Poythress's outstanding work in which he concludes that the *biblical* position, based on the example, ministry, and singing of Christ himself, is that congregational singing may include *any words that communicate the teaching of Scripture*.[13] He argues, from Ezra 3, that

> the essence of the regulative principle is that our worship must be in Christ: it is conformity in thought, word, and deed, heart, soul, mind, and strength, corporately and individually, to the sovereign, glorious, exalted ministry of Christ, as prophet, priest, and

king, at the right hand of God. We insist that we do not
go beyond Scripture, but with the wisdom of Christ
seek to understand Scripture, when we say that this
Scripture (as we have argued) enjoins us to sing with
both the 150 and other songs, as the needs of teaching may require.[14]

The psalms teach us how to worship, and they provide fitting, biblical language with which to thank, praise,
implore, and glorify God. They also demonstrate confession
and lament. Some are overtly messianic; others recount
Israel's redemptive history. A historical study of sung psalms
in the worship of the church reveals multiple traditions:
from Gregorian psalmody to the metrical psalms of Calvin's
psalters, to the early American *Bay Psalm Book* (1640), to
Anglican chant; and from the psalm-hymns of Martin Luther,
Isaac Watts, and James Montgomery to small- and large-
scale psalm settings by a great many composers. In other
words, the psalms must be sung, but the manner in which
they should be sung (language, medium, mode, music) and
their place in the liturgy are matters of some choice.

Canticles

Singing hymns of praise was the response of many biblical saints to God's deliverance and other blessings. Like
the canonical psalms, these biblical songs were recorded in
written form. Although the Old Testament includes laments
such as David's great elegy for Jonathan and Saul in 2 Samuel
1:17–27,[15] canticles typically rehearse the attributes of God
and his mighty acts on behalf of his people—specifically his
acts of *creation* and *redemption*. They give glory to God and
manifest a spirit of joy and thankful praise for his work and
deliverance. For example:

- Moses, Miriam, and all Israel sang after the nation was delivered from the hand of Pharaoh at the Red Sea (Ex. 15).
- Deborah and Barak sang when God gave victory to the Israelites over the Canaanites (Judg. 5).
- David sang as the Lord delivered him from the hand of his enemies and from Saul (2 Sam. 22).
- Mary sang upon seeing Elizabeth, who understood that God's promise of a Redeemer was going to be realized through Mary (Luke 1) [*Magnificat*].
- Zechariah sang following the return of his speech as he was filled with the Holy Spirit and verified his son's name—John, the one who would prepare the way for the Savior (Luke 1) [*Benedictus Dominus Deus Israel*].
- Simeon had a similar response when he held Jesus, the Messiah, in his arms, having entered the temple "in the Spirit" (Luke 2) [*Nunc dimittis*].

There are Old Testament songs of Jacob (Gen. 49), Hannah (1 Sam. 2:1–10), Moses (Deut. 32), and Habakkuk (Hab. 3), as well as numerous other *cantica minora*, in Exodus, Deuteronomy, 1 Samuel, 1 Chronicles, Isaiah, and elsewhere. The three New Testament canticles mentioned above are also known as the "Lukan Psalms," or *cantica majora*. They demonstrate the continued writing and singing of inspired Christian psalms, apart from apocryphal songs, after the compilation of the canonical psalms had concluded. Old notes that "these are clearly Christian psalms written in the literary genre of the Hebrew votive thanksgiving psalms. . . . The Old Testament psalms had for generations cried out for the Lord's anointed; now the New Testament psalms confessed that the cry had been heard and the promise fulfilled."[16]

These biblical songs were the response of Spirit-filled people to God's salvation. They are the Bible's evidence of an appropriate, enthusiastic, righteous way for God's children to respond to divine deliverance—to sing the gospel and recount God's acts and attributes. Gospel-centered churches preach Christ's work of redemption. The Scriptures sing this gospel time and again, and so should we, in joyful praise.

The *Magnificat* and *Nunc dimittis* are sung regularly in Vespers and Evensong services; these and other canticles reside in the Lutheran, Anglican, Orthodox, and Roman Catholic traditions in numerous places as service music. Perhaps their prominence in liturgical traditions is among the excuses for not employing them in less liturgical, evangelical or Reformed worship. Others exclude them because they are not part of the 150. But why would inspired Old Testament psalms be considered greater than inspired New Testament psalms, which respond directly to the revealed person of Jesus? Since these are Spirit-inspired biblical songs, all Christians would be well advised to sing them. Not doing so deprives us of some of the rich hymnody of the Scriptures.

Hymns of Christ

In addition to quotations from the Old Testament psalms and canticles, there are New Testament passages, particularly in the Epistles, with heightened poetic language and hymn fragments.[17] There is no conclusive way to distinguish between poetry and hymnody in the New Testament, since both contain the fundamental features of Hebrew poetry. Normally such biblical passages are Christocentric. They usually appear in modern Bible translations with indented margins, italics, or quotation marks that set them apart from the regular prose. Passages in Philippians 2 and Colossians 1 are hymns of Christ, which scholars think may be representative of Greek poetic forms familiar to the Greek-speaking congregations. Certainly the doxological hymns of Revelation 4 and 5 are hymns of Christ.

While one reads of Christ in the book of Psalms, that book focuses on the worship, attributes, and acts of God the Father more overtly than those of the Son, whose advent was still anticipated. The Gospel and Epistle passages, on the other hand, poetically celebrate the lordship of Jesus Christ and provide hymns specifically to and about Christ after his first coming—a new genre of biblical song. As Ralph Martin puts it:

> It was in worship that the decisive step was made of setting the exalted Christ on a level with God as the recipient of the church's praise. Hymnology and Christology thus merged in the worship of one Lord, soon to be hailed after the close of the New Testament canon as worthy of hymns "as to God" (Pliny's report of Bithynian Christians at Sunday worship, A.D. 112).
>
> It was this close drawing together of the persons of the Godhead which laid the foundation for the Trinitarian creeds, and raised a bulwark against classical Gnosticism in the late second century. . . . While "messianic psalms" played their role in defining and defending the church's belief in the fulfillment of Old Testament types and prefigurements, it required a new species—the "hymn to Christ"—to open fruitful avenues of Christological and soteriological inquiry that set the church from its early days on a course that led eventually to Chalcedon and the *Te Deum*:
>
> You are the King of Glory, O Christ,
> You are the everlasting Son of the Father.[18]

Watts's Contribution

Isaac Watts authored psalm paraphrases and hymns in a quest to "Christianize" the psalms. Like Luther, Watts wanted believers to benefit from psalm singing, so that it would not be an intellectually or culturally remote activity, but one from which they would learn. To facilitate this educational benefit, Watts abbreviated lengthy psalms and avoided potentially confusing metaphoric language. Further, he makes reference to Christ in at least one stanza in most of his paraphrases. For example, in the setting of Psalm 103, "O Bless the Lord, My Soul," the final stanza reads:

> His wondrous works and ways
> He made by Moses known,
> But sent the world His truth and grace
> By His beloved Son.

Another example is his paraphrase of Psalm 19, "The Heavens Declare Your Glory, Lord," where we find the stanza:

> Nor shall your spreading gospel rest
> Till through the world your truth has run;
> Till Christ has all the nations blessed
> That see the light, or feel the sun.

Watts wanted to make Christ's fulfillment of psalm prophecies evident: "In all places I have kept my grand design in view; and that is to teach my author to speak like a Christian."[19] He instructed congregants to carry psalm books with them and asked the clerk to read the psalm aloud before it was sung so that people might better understand what they were about to sing. In so doing, Watts restored Christian praise to its rightful place in the worship of the Dissenting Church of the early eighteenth century.[20] Understanding biblical principles of worship will have a similar restorative effect on the church today—it will enrich our worship and help guard against the dangers of relativism, Gnosticism, narcissism, and anthropocentrism.

Doxologies

The New Testament includes numerous excerpts from early Christian benedictions, prayers, creeds, eulogies, responses, and doxologies. Doxology encompasses the full gamut of praise to God and has been referred to as "the theology of worship."[21] Extended doxological passages occur in Romans 11:33–36 and Revelation 1:5–7, as well as in Revelation 4 and 5, 7:10–11, 11:15–18, 15:3–4, and 19:1–8. The five divisions of the canonical psalms each conclude with doxological passages, and Psalm 150 serves as a doxology to close the entire Psalter.

Romans 11:33–36. Romans 11:36 closes the opening doctrinal chapters of the book and acts as the climax of the apostle Paul's testimony. James Montgomery Boice put it this way: "As Paul contemplated the mercies of God, he was so lost in wonder that he composed the doxology . . . as an outpouring of praise—the song of the redeemed."[22] This doxology, which quotes Isaiah and Job, concludes that all things come both *from* and *through* God himself and lead rightly *to* the worship of God by his redeemed creation. This is the basis of a true Christian worldview. All things are to bring glory to God alone.

Revelation 4 and 5. There are five doxological hymns in Revelation 4 and 5, sung by the seraphim, cherubim, four living creatures, twenty-four elders, and all creation. The first two praise God the Father. The next two praise Christ the Lamb, and the fifth praises both the Father and the Son. God is worshiped for his holiness, for his everlasting existence, and for his creation. Christ is praised for his worthiness to open the seals and for his saving act of redemption. A "crescendo of praise" is evident in these hymns as well, as voices are added. The first is sung by the four living creatures, the second and third by the four living creatures and twenty-four elders, the fourth by the four living creatures, twenty-four elders, and myriads of angels, and the fifth by every creature in heaven and on earth and under the earth and in the sea.

This glimpse into heaven's worship informs our understanding of what worship should be after the death, resurrection, and ascension of Christ. As Old has pointed out, "One is struck by the fact that in Revelation's report of the heavenly worship there are constant echoes of the Psalms and canticles of the Old Testament and yet no example of a direct and simple use of one of the canonical Psalms. In every case what we have is a Christian paraphrase."[23] Since this is the revealed Word of God, and since it demonstrates at least a veiled picture of perfect, heavenly worship, such revelation is appropriate to imitate in gathered worship, with substantive music filled with the Christocentric praise of God.

WORSHIP MUSIC IS PRAYER

It Helps Us Approach God Rightly

By day the LORD commands his steadfast love, and at night his song is with me, a prayer to the God of my life. (Psalm 42:8)

A significant role of worship music is its role as a form of prayer. Subconsciously, I think, we tend to put singing and praying into separate categories. Perhaps this is because we engage in the former with open eyes, looking at words and notes, while we typically undertake the latter with closed eyes and bowed heads. In less liturgical churches, prayer is almost always extemporaneous, whereas songs sung in worship are prewritten. The Bible does not evidence this distinction—its prayers are written, as are its songs.[24]

Any communication to God (verbal or nonverbal, spoken, sung, written, or thought) is prayer. Communication does not cease when one sings, and yet somehow we separate singing from thinking, speaking, or "meaning." Perhaps this is tied in to the errant idea that prayer *must* be spontaneous—that unless it is improvisatory, it is not authentic or Spirit-directed. Certainly prayer can be spontaneous, but an aversion toward written prayer is incongruent with the fact that canonical psalms and other biblical songs are written prayers. These prayers have been read in worship in both ancient and modern times. Noncanonical written prayers will often be more substantial and biblical than those we extemporize, since they can be examined in advance for theological accuracy and can be crafted to express specific thought. We do not need to fear prayer in written form, but for it to be authentic we must believe and mean what we pray.

The reason that we have come to view prayer and singing so differently is uncertain, but the rise of music as entertainment within the church undoubtedly contributes to this phenomenon. How many spoken prayers end with applause, for example?[25] When music in church becomes entertainment, it is objectified as "an event." It turns into something to watch, a spectacle. Such events are detached from the immediacy of something in which we are actively involved. Other worship elements can be treated this way, too. Pastoral prayer can turn into an aural "spectacle" if members of the congregation are not praying along with the minister or if its delivery becomes more important than its content. Worship can become some-thing done *for* us instead of being done *by* us.

This disconnection is exacerbated by the music-suffused society in which we live (with music as a mindless backdrop for almost every other activity—shopping, dining, transpor-tation, sports, and so on). We become desensitized to music in public settings, as something in which we are involved neither as listeners nor as "doers." Musical alienation is a danger in services with soloists and choirs—the parishioner can come to view music as an event he is watching or to which she is listening as a bystander rather than as a participant.[26] Danger of alienation is just as prevalent, if not more so, in services with an ensemble of instruments and singers at the front of the church loudly rendering songs that are dif-ficult for the congregation to sing, resulting in two-thirds of the group watching words go by rather than actually par-ticipating. People may be involved tacitly, in that they may be standing, swaying, or clapping, but are they singing or praying? They might be, or they might not. Are worshipers with hymnbooks in hand thinking about what they are sing-ing or praying? They might be, or they might not. When we pray we *must* be mentally engaged (1 Cor. 14:15).

Music often serves as prayer, and prayer in the midst of the congregation is to be a group activity. Such is the case with the psalms, which served as the repertoire for the entire "congregation" of Israel. We need to find ways to engage the body of believers in prayerful music, whether it is a psalm, hymn, chant, solo song, choral anthem, or any other form.

Some Practical Suggestions

- Include musical texts being sung by choirs or soloists in the bulletin or Order of Worship. Not only will the congregation experience better textual clarity, but the printing of texts speaks to intention—one is *meant* to understand and participate in what is being sung.

- Pastors or other worship leaders can point out that the next song is a prayer or a hymn of praise to God for his redeeming work, etc.
- We should probably avoid using the terms *performance* and *special music* when it comes to music employed in worship.[27] A solo piece or anthem is more fittingly called a *musical offering*. It is not "special" if it happens every week. It is not more important than congregational song, and it certainly does not require applause. We must remember that what we sing is being sung to God.
- Hymns can be designated *Hymn of Thanksgiving*, *Prayer Hymn*, and so forth to help participants understand the music's purpose.
- If a church uses screens and a projector, the music should be included too, so that musicians can read it, and those who are less musically adept can at least have the opportunity to learn something about music; although I certainly prefer that worshipers have both text and music in their hands.
- An "Amen" can be sung at the end of musical prayers, further signifying their similarity to spoken prayer.

Direct Address

Many passages from the psalms, biblical canticles, hymns of Christ, and other songs, address God directly. Direct address is one of the most recognizable characteristics of musical prayer. The following are examples of hymns or choruses that address God directly:

- "Be Thou My Vision, O Lord of My Heart"
- "Holy, Holy, Holy! Lord God Almighty!"

- "My Jesus, I Love Thee, I Know Thou Art Mine"
- "Come, Thou Fount of Every Blessing"
- "Create in Me a Clean Heart, O God"
- "Speak, O Lord, as We Come to You"

Thinking of such songs as anything other than prayers is simply not supportable. There are prayer hymns addressed to each person of the Trinity:

- Father: "Dear Lord and Father of Mankind" (John Greenleaf Whittier)
- Son: "O Jesus, I Have Promised" (John Bode)
- Spirit: "Breathe on Me, Breath of God" (Edwin Hatch)

Calvin's View with Support from Scripture

Calvin understood the singing of psalms to be prayer, which aligns with the teaching of the last verse of the second book: "The prayers of David, the son of Jesse, are ended" (Psalm 72:20). "Spontaneous prayer only" rules out use of the inspired Psalter and other biblical songs. On the other hand, using only the canonical psalms excludes New Testament passages and examples from the early church, such as the Lord's Prayer or the "Sovereign Lord" prayer of Acts 4:24ff. Both fixed and spontaneous prayers are valid and supported by the example of Scripture.

Other New Testament passages relate singing to praying:

- First Corinthians 14:15 states, "I will pray with my spirit, but I will pray with my mind also; I will sing praise with my spirit, but I will sing with my mind also."[28]
- In James 5:13 we read, "Is anyone among you suffering? Let him pray. Is anyone cheerful? Let him sing praise."

Prayer and singing are closely associated in these passages, and *both* should be done with the spirit and with the mind.[29] In other words, we should *mean* what we pray with all our hearts, and we should *know* what we mean. We should also mean what we sing and know what we are singing. Lapses in intention or understanding have often rendered our singing and worship of God irrelevant, even irreverent. Both Calvin and Luther wanted worship to be direct and in the vernacular, which is why they fashioned psalms and hymns in French and German. But they did not make worship *simplistic* in the quest for simplicity; considerable substance, structure, and thought was involved.

We can unreservedly state that for Calvin, singing was prayer. He includes it as one of the three required elements of Reformed worship (preaching, prayer, and the sacraments). In the foreword ("Epistle to the Reader") to the 1543 *Genevan Psalter*, he wrote:

> As to the public prayers, these are of two kinds: some are offered by means of words alone, the others with song. And this is not a thing invented a little time ago, for it has existed since the first origin of the Church; this appears from the histories, and even Saint Paul speaks not only of praying by word of mouth, but also of singing.[30]

Errors, Implications, and Pastoral Choices

Most pastors have had little musical training and received no church music instruction in seminary. Without musical education, it is easy to accept pragmatic musical ideas around us—the example of what has worked for megachurches, what is suggested by church-growth "experts," or what an influential elder or wealthy member insists on. In hopes of bringing increased vitality to church, contemporary services are added, with psalms and hymns often demoted or excluded from worship. This flawed approach comes from the mistaken belief that growth in church attendance on the basis of popular musical style ensures spiritual growth. Another mistaken notion is that worship music's purpose is to attract the unsaved, and then the teaching ministry will take care of the rest. A third is that such changes are necessary "for the young people." Such errors are rampant.

At the root of these errors is the idea that worship music is predominantly a tool for evangelism. Reformed churches with conservative doctrine in their preaching ministry often "dumb down" their music in an attempt to make services more palatable or accessible to people. They may not do this with preaching, but they will with music, either unaware or not acknowledging that worship music exists for the *same* kinds of purposes as preaching and teaching, and not fully grasping that worship music's subject and object is God. Many pastors and churches would like to have good music, but they are willing to sacrifice it as long as the pulpit ministry is strong. This creates a double standard in our message. The gospel power of worship music is denied, and we wind up depriving our congregations of the rich depths of vibrant, biblical music ministry. Is it possible that our actions declare that what we offer people is more important than what we offer God?

Another error suggests that we are responsible for producing new means or methods to build the church—that we have to "package" the gospel in postmodern clothing. While men tend to build kingdoms for themselves, it is God who builds his church through the faithful preaching of his Word and the biblical worship of his people. God's ways are timeless, unchanging, and true. We must meaningfully interact with people immersed in popular culture, yes; but we do not have to take on its character or speak with its trendy musical accents. So often when this is attempted (when we try to sound fashionable), the result is an inferior version at which the world scoffs. In fact, the more *different* worship music is from popular culture, the clearer the alternative it offers to those seeking depth, peace, truth, and hope in a dark, pagan, and pluralistic consumer age.

Choosing Worship Music

Pastors may select congregational song, though this significant task is often delegated to others. Whoever fulfills this responsibility, the charge is an important one. As Old states in his book on worship for pastors entitled *Leading in Prayer*:

> Choosing appropriate hymns is an important part of leading the congregation in prayer. We may not always regard hymnody as prayer, but theologically that is how it makes the best sense. In hymns the people of God pray together with one voice. As Luke puts it in his report of an early Christian prayer meeting, "they lifted their voices together to God" (Acts 4:24). Luke actually says this about psalm singing, but the same is true of hymnody as well. Uniting our voices together is just what we do when we sing.[31]

If we truly comprehended that many of our hymns are prayers, might we approach them (and sing them) differently? When we sing psalms and hymns of the faith together, we are corporately praying not only in the present but also in solidarity with saints of the past who have uttered the same words. There is tremendous value in this heritage that, sadly, the postmodern church seems willing to dismiss.

Each song to be sung in worship should be examined for its biblical content *and* for its musical credibility (melody, harmony, rhythm, and form). In so doing, one should determine whether the piece is a prayer of confession, supplication, or adoration; or perhaps it is a hymn of praise, or a song of thanksgiving, or some other genre. Such ideas can be shared with those singing or listening and will also help determine where the music best fits in the service. This is an important step in making musical worship intentional. The music and text must also be congruent with each other.

Too often our congregations are unaware that they are praying in song, or that they are singing a psalm of confession, or that a particular hymn is creedal or doxological. Pastors should set the example in this regard, by teaching on the matter, and by participating in musical worship instead of thumbing through sermon notes, talking with another staff member on the platform, or staring vacantly into space while the congregation is being asked to worship God. We all need to participate when the church is praying together. We are all commanded to sing.

WORSHIP MUSIC IS PROCLAMATION

It Teaches and Preaches God's Truth

My tongue will sing of your word,
for all your commandments are right. (Psalm 119:172)

In present-day evangelical and Reformed churches of all stripes, many congregational acts of worship are regarded as preamble to the sermon. Music, in particular, appears to be a "lighter" element of worship than those that seem to be more spiritual, such as praying and preaching. This worship-element hierarchy does not exist in Scripture, and our thinking is more biblical when we understand that preachers and musicians actually share the ministry of the Word. Proclamation and interpretation of the Bible, and the edification and encouragement of the saints, with the ultimate goal of giving glory to God—these are goals of the pulpit ministry, but they are also purposes of worship music delineated in the Word of God and heralded by theologians and musicians throughout the history of the church.

Luther's View

Martin Luther championed the biblical idea that church music can teach and preach spiritual truth; this is summarized in his statement, "God has His gospel preached through music too."[32] Luther advocated the significant role that music could play in the spiritual growth of the Christian when he declared, "Music and notes, which are wonderful gifts and creations of God, *do help gain a better understanding of the text*, especially when sung by a congregation and when sung earnestly," and "We want the beautiful art of music to be properly used to serve her dear Creator and his Christians. He is thereby praised and honored and *we are made better and stronger in faith* when his holy Word is impressed on our hearts by sweet music."[33]

With composer and collaborator Johann Walter, Luther compiled and edited hymn collections, and for many of these he wrote prefaces. One goal, Luther explained, was to educate the youth of his day:

> These [hymns] are set for four voices for no other reason than that I wished that the young (who, apart from this, should and must be trained in music and in

other proper arts) might have something to rid them of their love ditties and wanton songs and might, instead of these, learn wholesome things and thus yield willingly, as becomes them, to the good.[34]

Luther's basis for musical proclamation was Scripture, where we find more than six hundred references to music. His aim in hymn writing was to put the "Word of God into song." In other words, he sought to teach the Bible through music—to create theological expressions in musical form. Luther had earlier encouraged a schoolmate to fashion biblical psalms into German verse "so that the Word of God even by means of song may live among the people."[35]

Six of Luther's hymns were for catechism. These included a hymn on the Ten Commandments, one for the Apostles' Creed, one for the Lord's Prayer, another for baptism, one for confession, and one for the Lord's Supper. The 1543 Lutheran hymnal printed in Wittenberg included another, following these standard six, the hymn *Erhalt uns, Herr, bei deinem Wort* ("Lord, Keep Us Steadfast in Thy Word"). The three doctrinal stanzas of this hymn reinforce Trinitarian teaching through the Father who preserves, the Son who defends, and the Spirit who unifies.[36]

In Lutheran hymnody, the Protestant doctrine of the priesthood of all believers was made obvious.[37] Every Christian could communicate with God through song without the need for an earthly priest to intercede. Just as Luther translated the Bible so that his people could read it in their own tongue, likewise he put hymnbooks in their hands so that they could sing in their own language. No longer was the music of worship limited to trained clergy or choirs, but now *every* believer could participate. Hymnals were a Reformation innovation. They are part of our heritage—something to be treasured and used, not something to be thrown out.

Bach's Musical Offerings

Johann Sebastian Bach provides the quintessential example of what a church musician can be. He has been called a "musical preacher," and his church music may be characterized as "hermeneutical." Georg Motz, Bach's contemporary, compared composers and preachers: "You only have to look at an honorable composition to detect exactly what you find in a good preacher. For he takes as much care to guide his listeners toward what is good as a musician stimulates his audience toward the same goal through different variations and motions."[38] Motz maintained that honorable church music possesses the qualities of a good sermon. Those who have experienced worship music aiding them in understanding biblical text will concur. Music can be powerfully used by the Spirit to inculcate truth into our hearts and minds. Sometimes we are moved by musical truth in such a profound way that words fail to describe the experience, but we know the Lord has worked through the music to help us.

J. S. Bach has been called a "second Luther" and even the "fifth Evangelist" for his heralding of the Gospels in his passions and cantatas. Martin Naumann wrote:

> The works of other great musicians speak to us, but the works of Bach preach to us. These sermons, his cantatas, and particularly his *St. Matthew Passion*, proclaim the glory of the God of the Bible in a thousand ways. . . . Bach had something to say by reason of his faith and . . . his office. He said it in a language that fits the grand theme. He preached Christ and Him crucified. He extolled the Son of God as the Savior of the world. That is why we may call him a preacher.[39]

Bach was a great student of Luther, owning three sets of Luther's commentaries, which were studied and copiously marked. Bach's stated goal was to compose "well-regulated church music to the glory of God."[40] His familiarity with Lutheran theology, coupled with his own classical education, intuition, and logic, allowed him to develop a musical language rich in rhetorical devices and hermeneutical designs.

In the Lutheran service of Bach's day, the cantata (the primary service music) followed the Gospel reading and functioned as a response to and interpretation of this liturgical reading.[41] To be more specific, the cantata illuminated the text as a "vehicle for the proclamation of the Gospel."[42] This manifested Luther's view that music should be employed "in the service of exegesis and of the enlivening of the Word" in order to "intensify the biblical text through melodic, rhythmic, harmonic, and contrapuntal means," allowing it to "strike the hearer in full force."[43] Bach understood artistic music to be part of the preaching and teaching ministry and never merely for the entertainment of the congregation or as an adornment to the liturgy.[44]

Of Christian composers who are mindful of their interpretive responsibilities it can be said:

> Thus righteous composers, using all their qualities for expressing every word of a text artistically in a religious composition, show sufficiently that they are not concerned only about sweetness, but also about religious matters as true Christians. And therefore a well-worded piece of church music consists not only of a melodious exterior, but even more of true holy devotion and meditation.[45]

How wonderful it would be if this could consistently be said of the church music being released by music publishing houses and composers today! But in a market-driven publishing world, sadly, what is selected to print is what will "sell," not necessarily what is wholesome or artistically enriching.

Bach's music not only proclaims, but also *invites* the parishioner to participate, confronting the hearer both musically and textually so that understanding is enhanced. Bach does not permit retreat into the distance as a bystander; rather, he involves the listener in thought and decision on an existential level.[46] The Word needed to be *heard* (*fides ex auditu*—"faith from hearing"; Rom. 10:13–14, 17), and so it was preached from the choir loft as well as from the pulpit. The cantata's concluding chorale often acts as application—restating or summarizing the cantata's biblical truth in the hymnic language of the people. Congregants knew these chorales as well as we know hymns such as "Amazing Grace" and "O Come, All Ye Faithful"; thus, using them in compositions held meaning for the congregation.

Hymns and psalms can be proclamatory, as we will discuss further. But in Bach's case, additional musical offerings in the service frequently served this role as well. Bach's cantatas have characteristics that would be appropriate for musical offerings in our churches:

- They were often newly composed or arranged (for the church he was serving) but were rooted in musical and liturgical tradition.
- They were intricately tied to the liturgy and to the sermon, functioning as a sermon in their own right and employing fine sacred poetry.
- They were a vital, planned element of worship in the service.
- They were artistic and complex, yet they connected with the people in that they made use of known hymns.

- They preached, meditated on, and interpreted the Word of God.
- They were Christocentric, not anthropocentric (Christ-centered, not man-centered).
- They engaged the congregation in both contemplation and response.
- They required thought but were also full of emotion.
- They manifested good form, musical logic, and beauty.
- They were functional, artistic music involving both professional and lay musicians. They were not commercial, pop, or folk music led by amateurs.

If we valued and revived those kinds of principles in our church music today, a much-needed modern reformation would take place in our worship.

Biblical Support for Music as Proclamation

Within the context of proclamation, we find exhortation, admonition, teaching, and doctrine. Colossians 3:16 states, "Let the word of Christ dwell in you richly, *teaching and admonishing* one another in all wisdom, singing psalms and hymns and spiritual songs, with thankfulness in your hearts to God." Singing, in particular, is advocated for instructing and exhorting one another. The Bible is unambiguous in stating that sacred music has a spiritual, educational purpose. Numerous psalms record the works of the Lord, so that these might be relayed by oral tradition from priests to people and from parents to children.[47] Psalm 60 even has the ascription "For Instruction." But clearly, all the psalms were to be taught and sung.

Singing the Word of God will strengthen one's understanding of it. Singing should, moreover, be a result of hearing and meditating on God's Word, as the psalmist said in the last section of Psalm 119, that great song of the Word:

> My lips will pour forth praise,
>> for you teach me your statutes.
> My tongue will sing of your word,
>> for all your commandments are right.
> . . . .
> I long for your salvation, O LORD,
>> and your law is my delight.
> Let my soul live and praise you,
>> and let your rules help me.
>> > (Ps. 119:171–72, 174–75).

Since singing can function as a biblical response to hearing God's Word, the singing of psalms, hymns, or other worship music rightly follows the reading, teaching, or preaching of Scripture.

Luther's Proclamatory Hymnody

Luther believed that the gospel was proclaimed both by the spoken word and by the sung word. He frequently employed the phrase "say and sing" or "sing and say" to describe this proclamation. In his foreword to the *Wittemberg Gesangbuch* 1524, Luther wrote:

> As a good beginning and to encourage those who can do better, I and several others have brought together certain spiritual songs with a view to spreading abroad and setting in motion the holy Gospel which now, by the grace of God, has again emerged, so that we too may pride ourselves, as Moses does in his song, Exodus 15, that Christ is our strength and song and may

not know anything *to sing or to say*, save Jesus Christ our Savior, as Paul says [1 Cor. 2:2].[48]

In his commentary on Psalm 118 we read:

> They [the righteous] praise only God's grace, works, words, and power as they are revealed to them in Christ. This is their *sermon and song*, their hymn of praise.[49]

One of his best-loved Christmas chorales, *Vom Himmel hoch*, puts it this way:

> From Heaven above to earth I come
> To bear good news to every home;
> Glad tidings of great joy I bring,
> Whereof I now will *say and sing*.
>   [*Davon ich sing'n und sagen will*].

Luther says that this singing and saying is the mark of a true believer—the mark of the gospel on his or her life. In his preface to a later hymnal, the Bapst *Gesangbuch* of 1545, he wrote:

> For God has cheered our hearts and minds through his dear Son, whom he gave . . . to redeem us from sin, death, and the devil. He who believes this earnestly cannot be quiet about it. But he must gladly and willingly *sing and speak* about it so that others also may come and hear it. And whoever does not want to sing and speak of it shows that he does not believe and that he does not belong under the new and joyful testament, but under the old, lazy and tedious testament.[50]

Luther's motto is the proper vocation of every believer—to speak and to sing the gospel everywhere we find ourselves.

Responsibilities of Proclamatory Music

Musical proclamation occurs through any piece that teaches or sets a passage of Scripture, recounts God's work, issues a call to repentance, or reminds us of God's promises. Many proclamatory hymns focus on the basic tenets of the gospel and the life available to us because of Christ's sacrifice. As with other worship music, the musical setting of these hymns must match the text in tone and character.

Since the gospel can be preached through music, and since biblical teaching can be recalled through music and appropriated, there is an obligation to ensure that this is done well. When music is like a sermon, its responsibilities and characteristics must be similar to those of a sermon. Many of the same criteria used to define great preaching and teaching can be employed to define great church music. For example, church music needs to be well prepared and presented (i.e., it takes rehearsal and skill). It requires unity, coherence, and form. It should be intelligible, poignant, encouraging, convicting, and so forth. We should search for trained musical leaders as we do pastors. When we plant churches, we should be sending a music director along with the new pastor. Church music should feed the people by teaching the Word of God, and its benefits are a work of the Spirit of God.

Thinking about music ministry today in such terms will change the nature of worship in the church. As Donald Hustad points out, "Though mainline evangelicals claim to be leaders in Scripture study, biblical research to determine worship practice seems to be at the bottom of their priority list."[51] It is time for that record to change. What is worship music? It is praise, prayer, and proclamation in musical form, conformed to biblical principles. What is it not? It is not man-focused, self-indulgent entertainment for utilitarian or pragmatic purposes.

CONCLUSION

In order for church music to serve the worship of God properly in its roles as praise, prayer, and proclamation, we must follow these principles:

1. We must measure our worship practices by the Word of God.

Scriptural models and values should inform our thinking, traditions, and practices in worship. Therefore, if we discover that any of these are in conflict with biblical teaching or principles, we must change. To make such a discovery, or to confirm that our musical worship is biblical, we must read and study the Bible.

2. We need to comprehend the pastoral nature of music ministry.

Music is not in competition with pastoral work; rather, it *is* pastoral work. It can provide many of the same kinds of spiritual care that pastoral ministry provides. Music can comfort, encourage, instruct, teach, proclaim the gospel, interpret Scripture, make application, and reach the soul. All of these are the work of the Holy Spirit. Therefore, when and where there are parallels, the parameters that one applies to ministerial staff should be applied to church musical staff, and those applied to sermons and prayers should be applied to church music.

Pastoral musicians, irrespective of title, should be qualified, trained, spiritual, mature, humble, accountable, and aware of their responsibilities. They should be afforded honor, respect, authority, and sufficient (even generous) remuneration. Likewise, assisting musicians should be skilled, devoted, prepared, service-oriented, and conscious of the roles they fulfill in worship. The music presented should be excellent, the best the congregation can offer, spiritual, joyful, thoughtful, intelligible, fitting, God-honoring, theocentric, properly rehearsed, live, instructive, functional, and artistic.[52]

3. We should ensure that our practices are informed by and patterned after these truths.

Music in worship cannot be conformed to biblical standards unless it is actively supported by the church leadership in word and deed and is adequately funded. Priorities in our churches need to demonstrate our care for people over programs and buildings, and for the worship of God above all. Practices and priorities need to be informed by our knowledge of what God has revealed to be important—rather than by the status quo, common opinion, or "the way it has always been." Our evaluation of what is good and appropriate in worship must be determined by scriptural principle, not by popular whim, trends, or traditions. We must ask ourselves three questions: (1) *Why* do we do *what* we do in the *way* that we do it? (2) *How* should we be doing it according to Scripture? (3) *What* will it take to make it so?

May God help us to evaluate, alter, support, compose, sing, and play worship music in a spiritual manner, according to the principles that his Word conveys, for his own glory.

NOTES

1   The author would like to thank Dr. RoseLee Bancroft, Dr. Samuel Hsu, Karen Magnuson, and Aaron Gottier for their helpful review of this

material. Portions of this booklet have been adapted from Paul S. Jones, *Singing and Making Music: Issues in Church Music Today* (Phillipsburg, NJ: P&R Publishing, 2006); Paul S. Jones, "Hymnody in a Post-Hymnody World," in *Give Praise to God: A Vision for Reforming Worship, Celebrating the Legacy of James Montgomery Boice*, ed. Philip Graham Ryken, Derek W. H. Thomas, and J. Ligon Duncan III (Phillipsburg, NJ: P&R Publishing, 2003); and Paul S. Jones, "Calvin and Music," in *Calvin and Culture: Exploring a Worldview*, ed. David W. Hall and Marvin Padgett (Phillipsburg, NJ: P&R Publishing, 2010).

2 Hughes Oliphant Old, *Worship That Is Reformed according to Scripture* (Atlanta: John Knox Press, 1984), 39–41.

3 Ibid.

4 We will not treat these verses in terms of a distinction between *psalms, hymns*, and *spiritual songs*, an idea that has been explored by numerous theologians and other authors. A case can be made for these three names' identifying different types of canonical psalms because in the Septuagint they identify various of the canonical psalms. A case can also be made for their identifying different types of musico-poetic forms (such as psalms, hymns, and choruses; or psalms, canticles, and odes; or canonical psalms, inspired hymns, and extemporaneous songs). See also note 5.

5 Anthony Cowley and Randy W. Harris, *A Diagram Defense of Psalmody* (Elkins Park, PA: Covenanter Reformation Press, 1993). The authors also argue that *psalms, hymns*, and *songs* are all three modified by the adjective *spiritual (pneumatikais)*, which suggests that these "songs" are given directly by the Holy Spirit, or in other words can refer only to inspired psalms. For a fuller discussion of possible interpretations of these verses, see appendix 1 in Barry Liesch, *The New Worship: Straight Talk on Music and the Church* (Grand Rapids: Baker, 2001), which gives four views based on emphases in the Greek (imperative, attendant, resultative, and instrumental/modal).

6 Wesley W. Isenberg, "Hymnody: New Testament," in *Key Words in Church Music*, ed. Carl Schalk (St. Louis: Concordia, 1978), 181.

7 Derek Thomas, "Who Was John Calvin?" in *John Calvin: A Heart for Devotion, Doctrine & Doxology*, ed. Burk Parsons (Lake Mary, FL: Reformation Trust, 2008), 24.

8 Hughes Oliphant Old, *Worship: Reformed according to Scripture*, rev. ed. (Louisville: Westminster John Knox, 2002), 43–44.

9   Hughes Oliphant Old, "The Psalms of Praise in the Worship of the New Testament Church," *Interpretation: A Journal of Bible and Theology* 39, no. 1 (January 1985): 32.

10 As quoted in ibid.

11 Hughes Oliphant Old, e-mail message to author, January 1, 2010.

12 Hughes Oliphant Old, *Patristic Roots of Reformed Worship* (Zurich: Theologischer Verlag, 1975), 252. The hymn section includes hymns on the sacraments, for evangelical festivals, for children, for morning and evening, on the New Testament canticles, on the Ten Commandments, on the Beatitudes, and so forth. Johannes Zwick's preface to this book is an important defense of this balance of psalmody and hymnody, Old says.

13 See Vern S. Poythress, "Ezra 3, Union with Christ, and Exclusive Psalmody," *Westminster Theological Journal* 37 (Fall 1974–Spring 1975): 74–93, 218–35. "The point is, Christ sings New Testament words as well as the 150 psalms. He sings not only to God but among the nations" (91).

14 Ibid., 232. Poythress clearly believes that music is part of the teaching ministry.

15 David wanted this elegy to be taught to the people of Judah, so he recorded it in the book of Jashar.

16 Old, *Worship* (1984), 44.

17 Referred to here are passages such as John 1:1–5, 9–11; Romans 10:9ff.; 1 Corinthians 12:3; Ephesians 5:14; Philippians 2:6–11; Colossians 1:15–20; 1 Timothy 2:5–6; 3:16; 2 Timothy 2:11–13; Hebrews 1:3; and 1 Peter 3:18c–19, 22.

18 Ralph P. Martin, "Hymns in the New Testament: An Evolving Pattern of Worship Responses," *Ex Auditu* 8 (1992): 34–42. (These are only two lines from the *Te Deum laudamus*, not the complete text.) Pliny the Younger wrote to Emperor Trajan that the Christians in the first age met on a fixed day of the week before the break of day and sang a hymn to Christ as God (*Letters*, book 10, 97).

19 Isaac Watts, *The Psalms of David Imitated in the Language of the New Testament and Applied to the Christian State and Worship*, as quoted in Horton Davies, *The Worship of the English Puritans* (Morgan, PA: Soli Deo Gloria Publications, 1997), 178.

20 Davies, *The Worship of the English Puritans*, 176.

21 See Hughes Oliphant Old, *Themes and Variations for a Christian Doxology* (Grand Rapids: Eerdmans, 1992). Old believes that doxology is the

theology of worship and that the Old Testament sounds five musical themes that are fully developed in the New Testament, specifically epiclectic, kerygmatic, wisdom, prophetic, and covenantal doxology.

22 James Montgomery Boice, *Romans: An Expositional Commentary*, vol. 3, *God and History* (Grand Rapids: Baker, 1993), 1410, 1466.

23 Old, *Worship* (1984), 32.

24 This does not mean that some biblical songs were not extemporaneous at first. Exodus 15 is a good example of spontaneous praise led by a Spirit-filled prophet.

25 Applause rarely, if ever, belongs in a worship service. For a fuller discussion and rationale for this statement, see the chapter entitled "Applause: For Whom Are You Clapping?" in Jones, *Singing and Making Music*, 18ff.

26 There are ways to guard against this danger. Musicians do not have to be front and center—that position can be left for the pulpit and preacher. In the Presbyterian church's roots in Scotland, the pulpit was typically elevated, while the musicians sang from the back of the church, usually in a balcony, with the possible exception of a precentor, who may have used a front lectern or lower podium/pulpit. Music is supposed to be heard, but it does not need to be watched.

27 The word *performance* may have some merited use for what occurs in worship, but not in the way in which we commonly interpret the word. For a good discussion of this topic, see the chapter entitled "Is Worship a Performance? The Concept," in Liesch, *The New Worship*, 121ff.

28 The NIV uses the personal pronoun "my" before "spirit" and "mind"; but this is not in the Greek, as it is in 14:14. Paul distinguishes between his own spirit and the Holy Spirit in 1 Corinthians 5:4, for example.

29 Paul seems to equate singing or praying "with the spirit" to mean in another tongue—basically, in a language or manner in which the other worshipers present would not be able to participate or understand. "If you are praising God with your spirit, how can one who finds himself among those who do not understand say 'Amen' to your thanksgiving, since he does not know what you are saying? You may be giving thanks well enough, but the other man is not edified" (1 Cor. 14:16–17 NIV).

30 John Calvin, "Foreword: The Epistle to the Reader," in *Genevan Psalter* (1543), as quoted in *Source Readings in Music History*, ed. Oliver Strunk

(New York: W. W. Norton, 1950), 346. See also Charles Garside Jr., "Calvin's Preface to the Psalter: A Re-Appraisal," *Reformed Music Journal* 2, no. 4 (October 1990): 126–28, which is reprinted from *The Musical Quarterly* 37 (1951): 566–77.

31 Hughes Oliphant Old, *Leading in Prayer: A Workbook for Worship* (Grand Rapids: Eerdmans, 1995), 321.

32 *Luther's Works*, American ed., vol. 54, *Table Talk*, ed. and trans. Theodore G. Tappert (Philadelphia: Fortress Press, 1967), 129. Full statement: "God has His Gospel preached through music too, as may be seen in Josquin." Josquin Deprès (c. 1440–1521), the Burgundian church composer to whom Luther was referring, was in fact Luther's favorite composer and almost his contemporary.

33 Martin Luther, "Preface to the Burial Hymns (1542)," in *Luther's Works*, American ed., vol. 53, *Liturgy and Hymns*, ed. and trans. Ulrich S. Leupold (Philadelphia: Fortress Press, 1965), 328 (emphasis added).

34 Martin Luther, Foreword to the *Wittemberg Gesangbuch* 1524, which was the first edition of Johann Walter's *Geystliches Gesangk Buchleyn*, as found in Strunk, *Source Readings*, 342.

35 Robin A. Leaver, *Luther's Liturgical Music: Principles and Implications* (Grand Rapids: Eerdmans, 2007), 27 (referring to Georg Spalatin and quoting *Luther's Works*, vol. 53, 221).

36 Ibid., 113.

37 Roland H. Bainton, *Here I Stand: A Life of Martin Luther* (Nashville: Abingdon Press, 1977), 269.

38 Georg Motz, *Die vertheidigte Kirchen-Music* . . . (Tilsit, East Prussia, 1703), 14–15, as quoted in Ulrich Leisinger, "Affections, Rhetoric, and Musical Expression," in *The World of the Bach Cantatas: Johann Sebastian Bach's Early Sacred Cantatas*, ed. Christoph Wolff (New York: W. W. Norton, 1997), 194–95nn10–12.

39 Martin J. Naumann, "Bach the Preacher," in *The Little Bach Book*, ed. Theodore Hoelty-Nickel (Valparaiso, IN: Valparaiso University Press, 1950), 14, 16.

40 Hans T. David and Arthur Mendel, eds., *The New Bach Reader: A Life of Johann Sebastian Bach in Letters*, rev. Christoph Wolff (New York: W. W. Norton, 1998), 60–61.

41 Don O. Franklin, "J. S. Bach and Pietism," part 8, "Bach in Leipzig: Cantata as Text," *Pietisten XII*, vol. 1 (1997): 9.

42 Richard Jeske, "Bach as Biblical Interpreter," in *The Universal Bach* (Philadelphia: American Philosophical Society, 1986), 89.

43 Günther Stiller, *J. S. Bach and Liturgical Life in Leipzig*, ed. Robin A. Leaver, trans. Herbert J. A. Bouman, Daniel F. Poellot, and Hilton S. Oswald (St. Louis: Concordia, 1984), 150.

44 Robin A. Leaver, *J. S. Bach as Preacher: His Passions and Music in Worship* (St. Louis: Concordia, 1984), 14.

45 Georg Motz, as quoted in Leisinger, "Affections," in Wolff, *The World of the Bach Cantatas*, 195.

46 Jeske, "Bach as Biblical Interpreter," 90.

47 Psalms 78, 105, and 136 come to mind. This was a form of instruction as well as worship, particularly tied in with the wisdom literature of the Old Testament. The Jewish feast of Passover and other high holy days also featured the use of songs in the celebration of deliverance and as reminder of God's works. Also, of the 4,000 Levitical musicians whom David set apart for temple service (males over the age of thirty), the 288 distinguished for their special musical abilities were teachers of the other 3,712, who in turn taught their own sons and daughters.

48 Martin Luther, Foreword to the *Wittemberg Gesangbuch* 1524, in Strunk, *Source Readings*, 342 (emphasis added).

49 *Luther's Works*, American ed., vol. 14, *Selected Psalms III*, ed. Jaroslav Pelikan (St. Louis: Concordia, 1958), 81 (emphasis added).

50 *Luther's Works*, 53:333, as quoted in Leaver, *Luther's Liturgical Music*, 88 (emphasis added).

51 Donald P. Hustad, *True Worship: Reclaiming the Wonder & Majesty* (Wheaton, IL: Harold Shaw, 1998), 101.

52 Persons interested in guidelines for selecting quality church music might read the chapter entitled "Criteria for Good Church Music," in Jones, *Singing and Making Music*, 276ff.

264.2
J785 W

LINCOLN CHRISTIAN UNIVERSITY

122

3 4711 00207 6729